Contents

Some words appear in the text in bold, **like this**. You can find out what they mean by looking in the glossary.

Maps and mapmakers

A map is usually a flat piece of paper showing some information about the land. Most maps show a "bird's eye view" of the land. This means that they show how the land looks from above.

Maps can show lots of different information. They can show Earth's **natural features**, such as volcanoes and rivers. They can also show things that humans have built on the land, such as factories and roads. Maps are really useful for seeing how an area has changed over time.

People use maps to help them understand places and locations.

What are maps for?

Maps of the world are useful for lots of things. Television news reports or newspaper stories about different countries often have world maps showing where these countries are. When we learn about different countries, it is helpful to see where these countries are compared to our own. World maps can show us countries that are near to us, and countries that are very far from us.

MAPMAKERS

People who make maps are called **cartographers**. Making maps is called cartography.

Mapping a globe

Earth is not flat. Instead it is a **sphere** – a round object, like a ball. Using a **globe** is the best way to look at a map of the world. All the countries and oceans are in exactly the right places on a globe.

There are some problems with using globes. They are difficult to carry around and store. You can't put globes inside books or newspapers. They are also usually more expensive than paper maps.

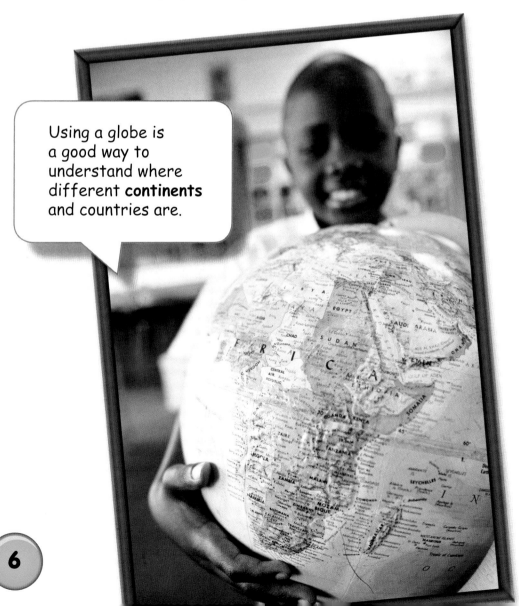

Using a globe is a good way to understand where different **continents** and countries are.

Flattened Earth

Flat maps are much easier to use than globes. When we look at flat maps of the world, we have to try to remember that the real world is a sphere. Cartographers use special ways of drawing to get all of the countries on to the flat paper. They have to stretch some areas, and squash other areas, to get everything to fit.

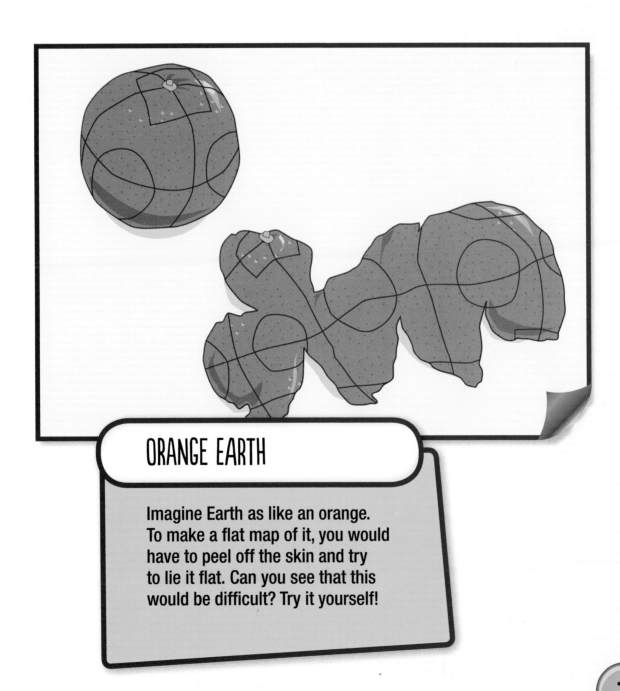

ORANGE EARTH

Imagine Earth as like an orange. To make a flat map of it, you would have to peel off the skin and try to lie it flat. Can you see that this would be difficult? Try it yourself!

Stretching the world

Many flat maps of the world try to show the correct shape of the land. This means that the sizes are often not correct. Maps that use a Mercator Projection have this problem. A **projection** is a way of showing a solid object on a flat surface.

Mercator Projection maps were first made in 1569. They show the shapes of the land, but the sizes are not accurate. Greenland looks almost as big as South America, when in fact South America is around eight times bigger!

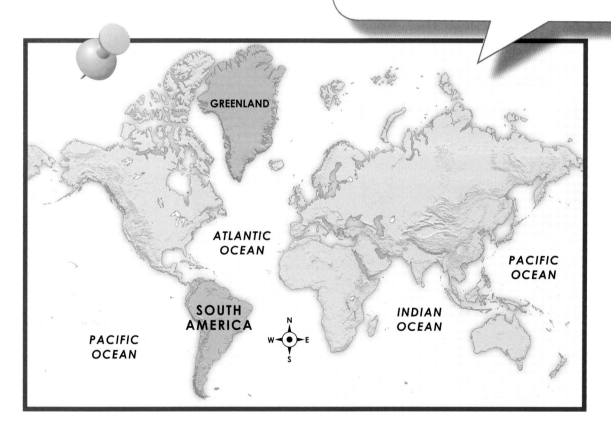

GREENLAND

ATLANTIC OCEAN

PACIFIC OCEAN

SOUTH AMERICA

INDIAN OCEAN

PACIFIC OCEAN

N
W E
S

Some cartographers have tried to make the land sizes more accurate. This means that the shapes have to be stretched. In 1885, James Gall created a map that showed the correct land sizes. In 1974, this became known as the Peters Projection, or sometimes the Gall-Peters Projection.

WINKEL-TRIPEL

In 1921, Oswald Winkel found a new way to show a world map. He tried to balance the problems of size and shape. This way of showing the world is used by many people now.

GREENLAND

SOUTH AMERICA

This is a Peters Projection world map. The sizes are more accurate – South America is much bigger than Greenland. But can you see how the shapes of the land masses have been stretched?

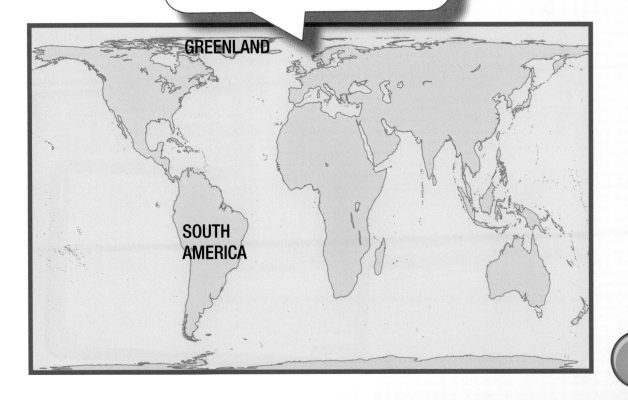

GREENLAND

SOUTH AMERICA

Lines around the world

Many world maps have lines running across and down them.
Lines of **latitude** are imaginary lines that go around Earth.
They are sometimes called parallels. The **equator** is the line of
latitude known as 0 degrees. The North Pole is at 90 degrees
North, and the South Pole at 90 degrees South.

Lines of **longitude** run from the top to the bottom of Earth.
They are sometimes called meridians. The **Prime Meridian** is
the line at 0 degrees. All the others lines are East or West
of the Prime Meridian.

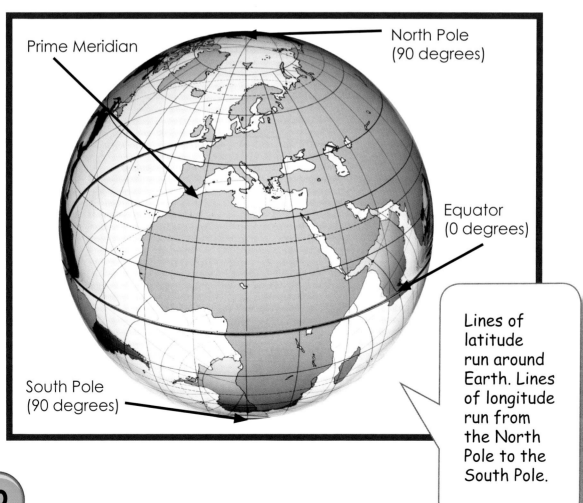

Prime Meridian

North Pole
(90 degrees)

Equator
(0 degrees)

South Pole
(90 degrees)

Lines of
latitude
run around
Earth. Lines
of longitude
run from
the North
Pole to the
South Pole.

Using the lines

Cartographers use lines of latitude and longitude to help them make flat maps of the world. By checking the positions of the lines on a globe, they can make sure that countries are placed correctly next to each other.

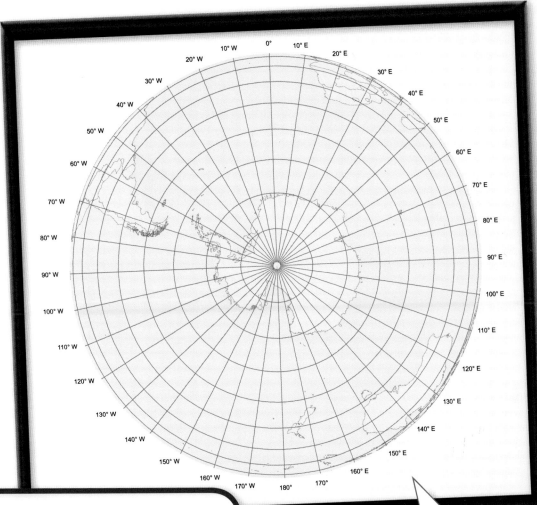

FLAT EARTH

Over 2,000 years ago, most people thought Earth was flat. Then the ancient Greeks guessed that it must be a sphere. They were proved to be correct when explorers sailed right round the world for the first time in 1519–22.

All lines of longitude meet at the South Pole (shown here) and the North Pole.

Pinpointing places

Finding places on Earth's surface is easier than you might think. We can use lines of latitude and longitude to give each place its own **coordinates**. Coordinates are made up of two numbers. The first is how many degrees of latitude the place is North or South of the equator. The second is the degrees of longitude East or West of the Prime Meridian.

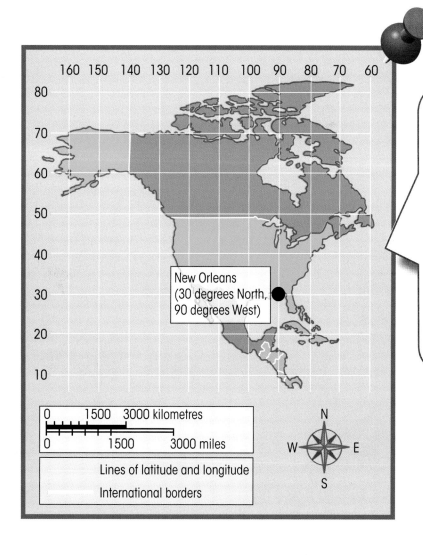

New Orleans
(30 degrees North,
90 degrees West)

0   1500   3000 kilometres

0   1500   3000 miles

Lines of latitude and longitude

International borders

This map of North America shows latitude and longitude lines. The city of New Orleans is located at 30 degrees North, 90 degrees West. These are its coordinates.

Between the lines

Places that don't lie on an exact line of latitude or longitude can still have coordinates. The distances between each line are split into 60 minutes. For example, Madrid in Spain has coordinates of 40 degrees and 10 minutes North, 3 degrees and 30 minutes West.

THE POLES

At the North and South Poles, all the lines of longitude meet up. This means that the coordinates are simply 90 degrees North for the North Pole, and 90 degrees South for the South Pole. There is a marker at the South Pole. These flags are at the South Pole.

The political world

Some maps of the world are political maps. Political maps show all the countries and the **borders** between them. Borders are usually imaginary lines separating two countries. Sometimes, borders follow natural features such as rivers or mountain ranges.

There can be borders inside countries too. Maps of different states, regions, or counties in a country can show the borders between them. Borders help people to understand which areas are under the control of which organizations and governments.

This map shows the countries that make up the continent of South America, and some of its major cities.

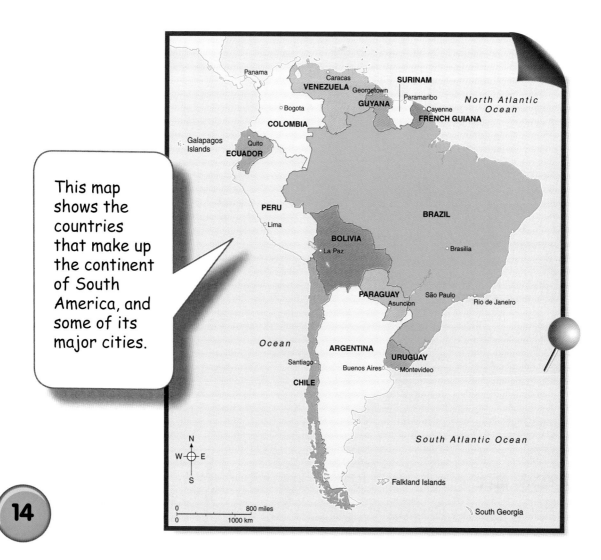

The world can be split into two halves, called **hemispheres**. The top half, north of the equator, is called the Northern Hemisphere. The bottom half, south of the equator, is called the Southern Hemisphere.

Unclear borders

Sometimes, not everyone agrees about the borders between countries. These are known as disputed borders. Countries on either side want to move the border and claim more land. There is often fighting at these borders to try to settle which country owns the land.

These residents of Thailand protest in Bangkok over the disputed border with Cambodia.

The physical world

Many world maps show the natural features of the land. These are called physical maps. They show things like major rivers and lakes, mountains and mountain ranges, and other land features such as deserts. They often ignore countries and their borders, and instead just try to show what the land is like.

Some physical maps use colour to show the height of the land. The lowest land is often coloured green. This changes to yellow, then orange, then brown, then purple, as land gets higher. Very high areas, such as the tops of mountains, are sometimes shown in white.

The world's highest mountains are the Himalayas in Asia.

Symbols

Some physical maps use **symbols** to show where certain natural features are. Symbols are little pictures or drawings. They represent things in real life. For example, a symbol of a tree might represent a forest. Maps using symbols also usually have a **key**. The key lists all the symbols and explains what each one represents.

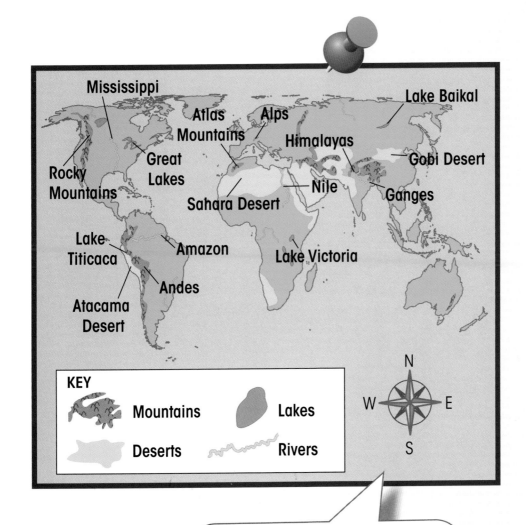

This map of the world uses symbols to show where different natural features are. Can you see the huge area of the Sahara Desert?

Water world

Mapping the world does not just mean mapping the land! Around 70 per cent of Earth's surface is covered in ocean. Is it important to have maps of the ocean as well as the land. Sailors need to know how deep the sea is, so they can steer their ships safely. Lots of the world's oil and gas comes from rocks under the sea, so oil and gas companies need to know where these rocks are.

This map shows the shape of the ocean floor around the world. Can you see that the ocean floor is not flat?

Ocean currents

The shape of the ocean floor can affect **ocean currents** around the world. Ocean currents are huge, moving bodies of water that flow in the same direction. They can be warm or cold, and they can affect the weather around the world. Maps can show the movement of these currents.

Arctic Circle
Kamchalka current
Alaska current
Labrador current
North Atlantic current
North Pacific current
California current
Kuroshio c.
Canaries current
Tropic of Cancer
N. Equatorial current
Eq. countercurrent
N. Eq. c.
Guinea current
N. Eq. c.
Equator
S. Equatorial current
Brazil c.
S. Eq. c.
Bengueta current
S. Eq. c.
Tropic of Capricorn
Peru or Humboldt current
Agothas c.
Falkland c.
West wind drift

KEY
Surface drifts and currents of the oceans
Warm currents ⟶
Cold currents ⟶

SEABED CHARTS

Sailors use detailed maps of the seabed, called charts, to make sure that their ships can move safely through the water. This prevents them becoming grounded on rocks or sand banks.

This map shows how warm and cold ocean currents move around the world. These currents can affect the weather.

How much detail?

Maps can't be as big as the area of land they are showing. Everything on a map is scaled down, or shrunk. World maps shrink everything down by a huge amount – the whole world is shown on one piece of paper! Other maps shrink everything a bit less. They might show a country, or a city. They can show more detail.

This map of Canada shows more detail than a world map could show. You could use this to plan a road trip around the country.

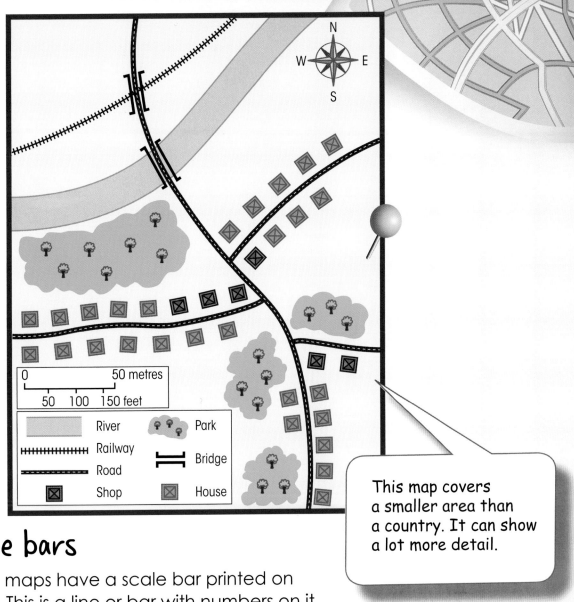

Key/Legend:
- River
- Railway
- Road
- Shop
- Park
- Bridge
- House

0 — 50 metres
50 — 100 — 150 feet

This map covers a smaller area than a country. It can show a lot more detail.

Scale bars

Some maps have a scale bar printed on them. This is a line or bar with numbers on it. You can measure something on the map and hold it against the scale bar to see how far something is in real life.

CHANGING SCALES

You will remember that it is difficult to show a sphere, like Earth, on a flat surface. The land has to be pulled and stretched to make the countries fit. Because of this pulling and stretching, world maps don't usually have a scale bar. This is because the amount of pulling and stretching is not even across the map. The scale bar would not be accurate for the whole map.

Old maps

People have been making and using maps for hundreds of years. Explorers made maps when they discovered new lands. They wanted to record the places they had visited.

In the past, people used **compasses** to help them make maps. Compasses have a spinning needle that always points North, so they help to work out directions. They also used **dividers** to work out distances, and **sextants** to work out latitudes.

This is called a sextant. Sailors used these to work out how far north or south they were of the equator.

Printing maps

As explorers went further into new areas, maps became more and more important. In the 1400s, printing was invented. This meant that copies of maps could be made, and so more people could own them. The first atlases (books of maps) were published in the 1500s.

ORDNANCE SURVEY

The Ordnance Survey is the UK's national mapping organization. It was set up in 1791, when the government decided to survey the south coast of England. It wanted to know the best places to build defences against any invasion.

Early cartographers drew maps of the world and printed them in books.

Satellites

Today, most maps of the world are made with the help of **satellites** that can take images of Earth with special cameras. This is called **remote sensing**, which means surveying something from far away.

Satellite images can show huge areas of land quickly and accurately. They can also show changes on the land surface over time. For example, the Aral Sea in Asia is shrinking, and satellite images can clearly show this.

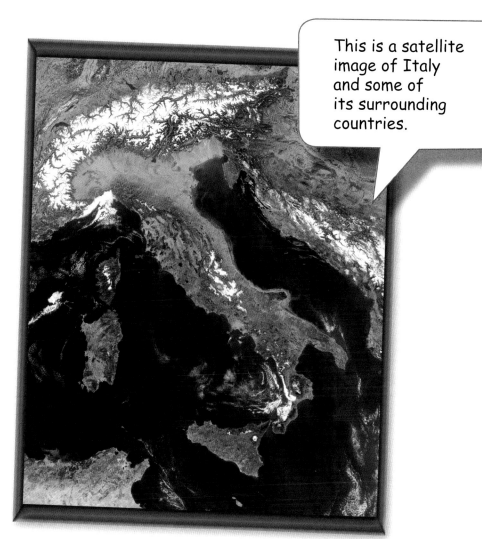

This is a satellite image of Italy and some of its surrounding countries.

Global Positioning Systems

There are 24 Global Positioning System (GPS) satellites orbiting around Earth. They send signals to equipment called **receivers**. The receivers can work out the exact coordinates for their positions on Earth.

Each receiver needs signals from at least three satellites to work out the coordinates. Receivers can be very small! Some mobile phones have GPS receivers built into them.

GPS FACTS

The first GPS satellite was sent into space in 1978. The full network of 24 satellites was completed in 1994. Each satellite lasts around 10 years before it must be replaced.

Using world maps

Map reading is a really useful skill. It is important to be able to read world maps so that you can understand them and find the information you need. The first thing to do when you look at a world map is to read the map's title or caption. Then you will understand straight away what it is trying to show you.

This is a globe of the world that shows South America. What do you think of when you think of a globe or world map?

Important steps in world map reading

- Try to learn roughly where your home town or neighbourhood is. It may not be marked on most world maps!

- Remember that a world map will show some areas a bit stretched or squashed, so they will look different on a globe.

- Stretching and squashing also means that most world maps don't have scale bars, so don't use them to try to measure distances.

- Make sure you look at the key so you understand what the symbols represent.

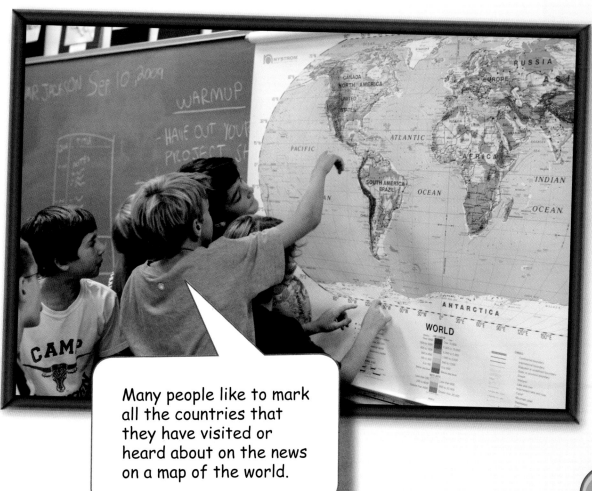

Many people like to mark all the countries that they have visited or heard about on the news on a map of the world.

Get mapping!

You will need a globe of the world and a flat map of the world to do this activity. You will also need some string and some sticky tape.

On your flat map of the world, find the city of Toronto in Canada. Now find the city of Nice in France. Tape the piece of string so that it connects the cities in a straight line. Now write down all the cities that lie along this piece of string.

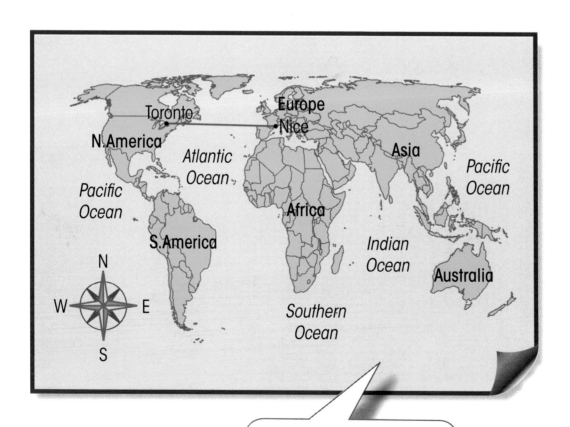

Use your flat map of the world and a piece of string to complete the above instructions.

Now find Toronto and Nice on your globe. Tape the string so that it goes from one city to another, following the shortest route around the globe. This is sometimes called a "Great Circle" route. Look at the cities the string passes through. Are they the same as the cities on the flat map?

Now compare the lengths of the string between the cities on the flat map, and on the globe. Which is shorter? Why is this? Which route do you think an aeroplane would follow?

How does the route between the two cities on your flat map compare with the route on your globe?

Glossary

border imaginary line that separates different countries, or different regions inside a country

cartographer person who makes maps

compass instrument with a needle that always points North

continent one of Earth's seven major areas of land, which are North America, South America, Europe, Africa, Asia, Australasia, and Antarctica

coordinates set of numbers that show a point on a map

divider instrument used to measure distances on maps

equator imaginary circle around Earth that is halfway between the North and South Poles

globe round ball with a map of Earth on it

hemisphere one of the two halves of Earth, either above or below the equator

key list of symbols and an explanation of what each one represents

latitude distance between the equator and a point North or South on Earth's surface; this distance is measured in degrees

longitude distance on Earth's surface that is East or West of the Prime Meridian; usually measured in degrees

natural feature something on Earth's surface that has been created by nature, for example a mountain

ocean current huge body of sea water that flows in the same direction, and can be warm or cold

Prime Meridian imaginary line on Earth's surface that goes from the North Pole to the South Pole

projection way of displaying an image on to a screen or flat area

receiver instrument which receives a signal from a satellite

remote sensing surveying something from a distance rather than actually measuring it up close

satellite spacecraft that travels around Earth and gathers or sends back information

satellite image picture, like a photograph, that a satellite can take of Earth from space

sextant instrument that uses the positions of the stars to help find directions

sphere solid, round object

symbol object or a picture that represents something

Find out more

There is a whole world of maps and mapping waiting to be discovered! Start by looking at some other books and websites.

Books

Collins Junior World Atlas, Stephen Scoffham (Collins, 2008)

Global Warming (Mapping Global Issues), Chris Oxlade (Franklin Watts, 2011)

Mapping Earth From Space (Science Missions), Robert Sneddon (Raintree, 2011)

Understanding World Maps (Maps and Mapping Skills), Meg Gillett and Jack Gillett (Wayland, 2012)

Websites

mapzone.ordnancesurvey.co.uk/mapzone/index.html
This is an interactive website all about maps and mapping, with homework help, maps, photos, and games. The teaching resources section includes lots of useful sheets about map skills.

www.oxfam.org.uk/education/resources/mapping_our_world/ mapping_our_world/l/home/index.htm
On this website, you will find puzzles and games as well as some different kinds of maps.

www.rethinkingschools.org/just_fun/games/mapgame2.shtml
Test your knowledge of some of the world's countries! This game asks you to click and drag the correct country name to the correct place on the map. The countries are all in North Africa and the Middle East.

www.worldatlas.com/webimage/testmaps/maps.htm
On this website, there is a section called Map Tests. You can print off lots of different maps, each one asking you to try to name the countries. The answers are given on a separate web page!

Index